"I CONFESS"

*To the many penitents who have been teaching me
how to be a better confessor*

"I CONFESS"

The Sacrament
of
Penance Today

Francis J. Buckley, S. J.

AVE MARIA PRESS
Notre Dame, Indiana 46556

Nihil Obstat: John L. Reedy, C.S.C.
          Censor Deputatus

Imprimatur: Most Rev. Leo A. Pursley, D.D.
          Bishop of Fort Wayne/South Bend

Library of Congress Catalog Card Number: 72-80971
International Standard Book Number: 0-87793-048-1

Published 1972 by Ave Maria Press, Notre Dame, Indiana

Photography: Pages 8, 48, 66 Anthony Rowland
                    20 Paul M. Schrock
                    38 Vern Sigl
                    60 Terry Barrett
                    76 Jean-Claude Lejeune

Printed in the United States of America

Contents

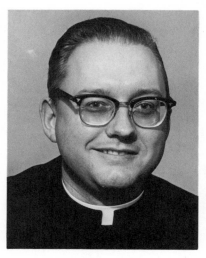

FRANCIS J. BUCKLEY, S.J., was born in Los Angeles, California. A graduate of Gonzaga University, he studied at the Pontifical Biblical Institute and the Gregorian University in Rome, where he received a doctorate in Sacred Theology. He is presently professor of Dogmatic and Pastoral Theology at the University of San Francisco.

Father Buckley has published articles in a wide variety of religious and scholarly journals, including *Word and Worship, Homiletic and Pastoral Review, Theology Digest, The Bible Today, America, American Ecclesiastical Review,* etc. He is the author of *Children and God: Communion, Confession, Confirmation* (Corpus Books); coauthor of *The Good News and Its Proclamation* (University of Notre Dame Press), the *On Our Way* series, and the *New Life* series (Sadlier); as well as coeditor of the *Faith and Life* series (Bruce).

PART I

The Penitent and the Confessor

1 What Happens in Confession?

1. If God forgives before confession, why bother to confess?

2. Is sin only a personal affair between the sinner and God?

3. How do "hidden" sins harm others?

4. What is the purpose of confessing in a confessional?

5. What are the advantages of confessing face to face in a lighted room?

6. What is the value of communal Penance services?

7. How can they be improved?

8. Can they replace private confession?

"I hate to go to confession. It's so boring!"

"I go to confession every week, whether I need it or not."

"I stopped confessing long ago. It may be all right for children, but I did more than my share in grammar school."

"I feel better after I've been to the sacrament. Sort of relieved. And it gives me strength to face the future."

"I can still remember my first confession. What a

nightmare! I'd forgotten how to begin and was kneeling there in the dark, frozen stiff, when I heard this disembodied voice, 'Well, have you anything to say?' It took me a year to get up enough courage to go back."

The sacrament of Penance means many things to many people. Some parents and teachers lack enthusiasm for it. For them it is a mechanical routine or an escape from guilt. Some priests consider it a chore and a bore, a waste of their Saturday afternoon or evening. Given these attitudes on the part of those who will introduce them to Penance, how can children be expected to discover or appreciate the unique value of this encounter with the forgiving Christ? Any preparation of children for the sacrament of forgiveness must start with the adults who will shape their experience.

Fortunately, some Christians look forward to confession as one of the high points of their week or month, and leave the confessional with a smile on their lips. There are priests who consider their hours in the confessional as among the most precious moments of their lives.

What secrets have they discovered about Penance? What happens at confession for them? What does the sacrament mean? What does it do?

PENANCE AS PROCESS

The sacrament makes visible a process which began long before the priest said the words of absolution or even opened the slide to listen to the penitent. The grace of Penance was at work from the first moment when the sinner became aware of his sin as a sin and felt ashamed. His desire to examine his conscience and to discover how and why he had gone astray; his sorrow at having devalued God and cheapened himself; his determination to set things straight and his first steps to make up to others for what his sins have done —all of this was due to the grace of God. God never writes off the sinner as a hopeless case, but takes the initiative to recall him to his senses. He can do this in countless ways: a word of reproach from a friend who was hurt, a word of encouragement from the gospel or liturgy, the pricking of conscience, the experience of the results of sin in disillusionment and frustration, isolation and loneliness. The Good Shepherd goes after the lost sheep to find him and coax him back. The return to God is indeed man's choice, but a choice preceded and accompanied by God's help. Once that choice is made, the sin is forgiven.

But if God forgives at the moment of repentance, what is the point of confession? This question opens up an avenue to understand the special nature of this sacrament.

All the sacraments make visible man's encounter with God, but no other sacrament can make so clear the dialogue-structure of the encounter. Penance alone takes the shape of a free-flowing conversation which can begin on one level but gradually peel off layer after layer of obstacles and defenses until the core of personality stands open before the gaze of God and self.

DIALOGUE: IN THE CHURCH

This dialogue between God and man takes place in a Church setting. The confessional is located in or near the church building. Even if the confession takes on the appearance of a counseling situation in the rectory parlor or chaplain's office, the confessor is a man of the Church. This serves as a reminder that the sinner finds God in and through the Church. He does not approach God in isolation but as part of a community, a family gathered around God's Son as his brothers and sisters.

His sins, whatever they are, have damaged his relations with God's people. His refusal to love has weakened the life-force of the body of Christ. He has discouraged others, has given a countersign of selfishness instead of Godliness, has made the Church less holy and less attractive. Any mortal sins would have excluded him from the Eucharist, the sign and source of Church unity and the food necessary for healthy Christian growth.

Yet his brothers and sisters have not rejected the sinner. The Church shares God's concern for him. The entire family forms a Church of sinners, all of us recognizing sin in ourselves and grateful for God's mercy. The priest as a man of the Church welcomes the sinner back in the name of God's people and invites him to take part in the eucharistic banquet. Once reconciled with God, he can take his place in God's family once again, sharing in the healing power of Christ and the holiness of the Spirit.

DIALOGUE: GOD TO MAN

God speaks to men in many ways, but more mysterious and impressive than any other is the way God speaks to men through other men. "Whoever hears you hears me," said Jesus (Lk 10:16). In the sacrament of Penance as in the incarnation the human voice becomes God's voice. Through the tone of voice and choice of words of the priest God shows his continual interest and loving care.

The priest in the sacrament is a man of God. His attention, his desire to listen and understand, his feel for the shame and humiliation experienced by the penitent reveal God's tenderness and solicitude. His respect enables the sinner to face up to his sinfulness and weakness in an atmosphere of acceptance. No matter what sins may have been committed, no matter how long since the last confession, the priest will not reject the sinner or turn away from him. His attitude becomes a symbol of God's constant and reliable love. He prolongs the presence of Christ the priest, who came to welcome sinners and give them new life.

As a man of God the priest helps the penitent face the future as well as the past. Out of their discussion the sinner can discover how to undo the harm done and the scandal given. The penance assigned can build on these insights, deepening his awareness of the presence and power of sin in life and its effects on him and those around him. A penance adapted to the sins confessed and the dispositions and state of life of the sinner not only purifies from the past by re-establishing the order shattered by sin; it also prepares for future decisions by alerting man to genuine values and building up good habits.

For example, Bill missed Mass on Sunday out of laziness. The proper penance for him might be to attend Mass during the week to atone for the damage done to the Church by his absence, or perhaps to get up early one day to perform an act of charity for someone who needs it. Rita missed Mass because she does not grasp its meaning or value. To oblige her to attend more Masses will not dispose her better but alienate her. Yet she might profit from reading a short explanation of Mass or from analyzing the structure of the liturgy or reflecting on some of the eucharistic prayers.

A judiciously chosen penance can enable the sinner to be more aware of what it means to participate in the redemptive work of Christ. It can prepare him to endure pain in the struggle to establish a social, economic, and political order characterized by justice and love.

Finally, the words of absolution express God's forgiveness, whether pardon has preceded the actual confession or not. God wants to reassure sinful man of his mercy, reconcile him to himself, and share with him his peace.

DIALOGUE: MAN TO GOD

From the penitent's side, his coming to confess expresses his faith that he can find God in the priest and can intensify his union with God through this man who shares the mediating function of Christ. Confession is a sign of his trust that all is not lost, that growth is still possible, that he has not been abandoned by God and the Church but can rely on their presence and support in his efforts to improve. Sincere acknowledgment of guilt results from an earnest look at self, a recognition of failure, a searching for reasons rather than excuses for bad decisions and behavior.

When fear of punishment motivates repentance, that very fear itself can be a move toward reality away from a fantasy-world in which the sinner thinks he knows better than God what is truly for his own good. If fear does not merely spring from a desire to do whatever is necessary to escape the consequences of sin; if it includes a "revaluation of values," replacing self with God as the supreme value in life and accepting responsibility for one's actions, such an attitude contains a fundamental love and reverence for God. Far better, of course, is a personal attachment to God so deep that the feeling of shame at sin flows not from the blow to one's self-image but from a sense of having been disloyal to one who has been constantly loving. The best disposition for forgiveness is one of love for God for his own sake, shifting attention from self to God and focusing on his inner goodness and lovableness rather than on what he has done or will do for the sinner.

One of the special characteristics of the sacrament of forgiveness is that it can change the disposition of the penitent. As the dialogue progresses, the original attitudes, which may have been quite self-centered, begin to be purified. The humility required to own up to guilt strikes at the very roots of pride. As more and more signs of God's love and reassurance of his pardon are perceived, the initial faith and hope grow and in turn intensify the response of love. Imperfect sorrow gradually becomes more perfect. No wonder then that some penitents experience intense joy at the end of confession! They have encountered the God of love and he has transformed them. He has listened and replied. He has understood and forgiven. He has renewed and deepened their friendship.

OTHER SYMBOLISMS OF PENANCE

Scripture often speaks of repentance or conversion as a process of illumination, moving out of darkness into light. "The people that lived in darkness have seen a great light. On those who dwell in the land of death's shadow a light has dawned" (Matt 4:16). "You were once darkness but now you are light" (Eph 5:8). "God has called you out of darkness into his wonderful light" (I Pt 2:9). From this viewpoint there is something to be said for the confessional box where distractions are removed and the penitent can concentrate on the darkness at the center of his heart. At the end of confession he steps from the shadows out into the light of the Church.

When ashamed, we are often afraid to face others. We lower our eyes, bend our heads, even hide our faces in our hands. For many Catholics anonymity in the confessional is precious. Without it they would be unable to confess.

The anonymity of the confessional can also symbolize the facelessness and isolation of someone who has refused to recognize himself as he is with his responsibility to others. But after he has discovered his true self and been reconciled to the community through the community representative, the priest, the forgiven sinner no longer remains in obscurity; he can enjoy the recognition and acceptance of his fellow Christians.

Jesus often used miracles of healing the blind or crippled to point to the blinding and crippling effects of sin. Physical healing can also point to the spiritual healing process of Penance. The patient goes to a trusted physician in hope of a cure, and to facilitate the diagnosis he tries to describe his symptoms in detail. His family physician should be already familiar with his personal medical history and know which medicines have been helpful, which have triggered allergic reactions. Or under the promptings of his regular doctor he may consult a specialist for a particularly serious disease.

Confession is also a learning situation. Christ the teacher through the priest teaches the sinner something about God and himself and mankind in general. From the experience of the past he draws lessons for the future.

In short, the sacrament of Penance is a rescue operation, by which God frees man from loneliness, isolation, weakness, ignorance, and fear—from the radical sinfulness which lies behind particular sins and is reinforced by the cumulative effects of sins. God saves the sinner from himself and restores him to the Church, where in an atmosphere of security, acceptance, and love man can grow to the full stature of Christ.

COMMUNAL PENANCE SERVICES

Penitential celebrations have a special significance of their own. Like the public penance practice of the early Church they can highlight the social nature of sin and the Church's role in pardon. But to achieve the full potential of such communal celebrations it is not enough that many individuals gather for examination of conscience, confession, and song.

Attention must be directed to the failure in social responsibility. Those within the Church were deprived of the good example to which they had a right. They were deprived of help which the sinners could have given them. They were perhaps even enticed to sin by the words or actions of those who as fellow Christians should have been solicitous for their union with God. Those outside the Church were put off by their sinful behavior. At the Last Supper Christ had said, "By this will all men know that you are my disciples, if you have love for one another" (Jn 13:35). Lack of love, then, will obscure the Church in men's eyes and make it harder for them to recognize God's people.

It is important that the group confront common problems, engage in prayer with and for one another, and reach communal decisions to engage in joint action in order to remedy bad social situations. Then it will be operating as a church, a community, and the experience of shared commitment and action will reshape attitudes and behavior for the future. After the scripture reading there could be a time for silent reflection, followed by discussions in small groups as to what should be done. This discussion itself could be the penance. Some sign of peace and fellowship could be exchanged before absolution.

By reflecting on the meaning and purpose of the sacrament outlined above—better yet, by changing the way they confess so that the meaning and purpose become more evident—ordinary Christians can improve their own attitudes to Penance and discover its power to bring peace and joy.

TO DISCUSS AND SHARE WITH OTHERS

1. *What would you say to someone who tells you, "I just ask God to forgive me. I don't see why I have to tell my sins to anyone else"?*
2. *Have you ever had the experience that Penance changed your attitudes or dispositions? How?*
3. *Have you ever experienced real joy after confession? Why?*
4. *How often should the average Catholic adult confess?*

2 How to Improve a Good Confessor

1. *What are the advantages and disadvantages of getting spiritual direction in confession?*
2. *What are the benefits of having a regular confessor?*
3. *What kind of "penance" would be more meaningful: a prayer or an action? Why?*
4. *How can penitents help the priests to be better confessors?*

If the sacrament of forgiveness is to be a dialogue, and if the effect of the sacrament hinges on the quality of the conversation and its impact on the disposition of the penitent, how crucial becomes the role of the confessor! So much depends on the way he carries on his side of the dialogue. He can conceal God or reveal him.

During the last few years there has been a sharp drop in confessions: about 50 percent in Europe and up to 75 percent in some parts of the United States. Churches that used to have long lines outside the confessionals on Saturday afternoon and evening and before First Friday now are empty. Why do so few take the opportunity to meet the God of forgiveness in this sacrament?

SOME CAUSES FOR DECLINE IN CONFESSIONS

For one thing, there has been a loss of the sense of sin. Many who used to have clear ideas of right and wrong are confused. There are so many conflicting voices telling them what to do or avoid that they find it hard to decide and many no longer care. Instead of turning to God in prayer for light, instead of searching their hearts to find hidden traces of self-deception and pride, how much easier to watch a football game or lose oneself in distractions.

A new concept of man, emerging from the psychological research of Freud and Jung, has led people to accept imperfections as human, not sinful or guilty. Love and hate, seduction and aggression, lurk below the level of consciousness and motivate almost all human behavior. Modern man has learned not to worry about this, but to harness the potential dynamism of these drives for good. Decline of guilt feelings has relieved the pressure which used to push many to confess.

Sins of omission and social evils like racism and pollution of the environment and oppression of the poor have become more important in adult consciousness. But the responsibility to do something about this is spread so thin that few feel compelled to have recourse to Penance. It seems more sensible and effective to write a Congressman or join Common Cause or the Sierra Club.

Giving these indirect causes their due, there remain other causes more directly responsible.

At a recent clergy conference, when the speaker mentioned the decline in confessions, the priest sitting next to me leaned over and said, "I wish the rest would stop coming, too!"

Some priests in the pulpit and others in the confessional have begun telling people not to confess unless they have committed mortal sin.

A magazine cartoon showed a lady kneeling at a confessional. On the other side of the screen was a huge machine with whirring tapes and flashing lights; and at the end of her confession the computer presented her with a printed card: "For your penance say three Our Fathers and three Hail Marys."

All of these point to a common problem. If priests do not appreciate the value of this sacrament, or if they administer it badly, they can kill its joy and make it a burdensome task and a mechanical routine.

Confession is the time when most priests have their closest contact with the majority of their people. Unlike a sermon, words in the confessional can be directed to one person alone with his unique problems. The penitent is giving his full attention, free of distractions. Because of the atmosphere of secrecy and intimacy, deep self-revelation becomes possible in a very short time, facilitating a very intense process of communication. Yet all of these opportunities can go for nothing if the priest is not prepared to take advantage of them.

Young seminarians need a far better training to be confessors and many of the other clergy will have to be retrained—if not by the bishop, then by their own penitents.

TRAINING A GOOD CONFESSOR

Most priests in the past were trained according to the axiom, "You must not make the sacrament of Penance odious or distasteful. Therefore, say as little as possible." The first principle is good; sacraments should be attractive. But the conclusion is no longer sound, if it ever was. The sacrament of Penance has been made unattractive by confessors who speak too little, forgetting the specific nature of this sacrament, which is an encounter with God's mercy and his concern for the sinner's spiritual growth. Nobody is going to get a deep sense of God's concern when confession of guilt is met by stony silence—followed by, "and for your penance say one decade of the rosary."

Moral theologians in discussing the sacrament of Penance say that the confessor should act as father, teacher, doctor, and judge. But most actual training in the seminary has centered on being a judge: how to distinguish mortal from venial sin, objective from subjective guilt, laws of God from laws of Church. All of this is good and valuable, but it has tended to make the sacrament too legalistic, cold, and impersonal. Penance was often understood by people as a mechanism to relieve guilt rather than a gift of God to create and intensify joy. When Jesus forgave sins, the evangelists do not say that the sinners were "relieved." They do say that they were full of joy. Zacchaeus in a burst of enthusiasm paid back fourfold for what he had taken unjustly and gave all his property to the poor (Lk 19:8). The parables of the lost sheep and lost coin and prodigal son all highlight the joy of restoration and forgiveness. It is a time to celebrate!

THE CONFESSOR AS DOCTOR

How can the confessor act as a doctor? Certainly he must diagnose the disease and treat it. But preventive medicine is better than radical surgery. If there is no real dialogue, no attempt to understand the person but only the situation, he is not going to detect the early signs of danger and prescribe the right remedy.

A good doctor needs a medical history. He needs to know the patient well, his past weaknesses and strengths, what medicines have helped him or been useless or produced counterreactions.

A doctor should not be disgusted by disease but respect the beauty and dignity of the life which is attacked by infection. He knows that the results of the treatment are not due to him alone but to forces of life which transcend his understanding and control.

By the words and actions of the confessor God heals the wounds of sin through love. The priest reveals the mercy of God to the penitent; or rather, he permits God to heal through him and reveal himself through him.

The counselor, too, is a kind of doctor, dealing with problems not purely physical. Some theologians have considered counseling itself to have a sacramental character, at least when the problems discussed have a religious or moral dimension. At any rate, the priest can learn much from the counselor about how to listen with full attention and without condemnation, how to convey an attitude of acceptance and hope, how to enable the penitent to see more clearly his responsibility and the need to change. In the acceptance and help of the counselor, God's forgiving grace is present and experienced more profoundly than in a bored recitation of a stock formula of absolution.

THE CONFESSOR AS TEACHER AND SPIRITUAL DIRECTOR

The role of a doctor is negative, an attack on the evil which confronts man and undermines his health. The role of a teacher is more positive, leading toward truth. Both roles are correlative in the spiritual order, for death to sin is a rebirth to life and to step away from sin is to step toward God. But of the two, the teacher's role is more important because of its positive thrust. Christianity should not be characterized chiefly by backing away from sin but by striding toward the outstretched hands of God. An essential function of the sacrament of forgiveness is to overcome the effects of sin so that the sinner can advance freely and confidently in the journey of life. For this he needs directions and guidelines.

Every sacrament is a teaching situation, a learning experience, because every sacrament is an encounter with God, and every real encounter involves communication, a mutual give-and-take, an opening of mind and heart to each other. But Penance lays particular stress on teaching because conversion demands a change of attitude. The set of values which led to sin must be rethought, new values must be discovered, old values rearranged in importance.

The penitent often comes because he does not know what to do. He wants to discern God's will for him, to make a fundamental choice which will affect thousands of his deliberate and free decisions later in life. He wants advice to control his emotions or break a habit. He wants someone to help him discover the hidden motives which lie behind his actions. All of this is a form of spiritual direction which can take place more rapidly and effectively in confession, where so many defense mechanisms are disarmed.

The confessor helps people form their consciences on war and peace, decent wages and foreign aid, sexual morality and civic duty. He can move attention from external facts to fundamental responsibilities: conscientious work on the job, honesty in business, respect for other members of the family, communication across the generation gap, authenticity in prayer.

The priest should give reasons behind Church laws

so that people can obey intelligently and explain their actions to others. No law of the Church is purely arbitrary. Some people have the impression that the Ten Commandments are God's law and bind everywhere and always, but that Church laws are arbitrary and admit exceptions. Such thinking does justice neither to the complexities involved in the composition of the Ten Commandments nor to the wisdom incorporated in Church laws. This authoritarian approach to law focuses attention on the lawgiver rather than the purpose of the law. All law derives its binding force ultimately from God, but God wants law because it organizes human behavior to achieve the common good. Crimes are bad not simply because they are forbidden by God; God forbids them because they are bad or harmful to those he loves.

Church laws are not arbitrary impositions from the outside; they do not add new obligations but specify the existing ones.

It is not arbitrary, for example, that Christians attend Mass on Sunday—as if the Church could make a law forbidding Sunday Mass. Why then does the law exist? God saves men not in isolation but community; he summons his family members to express this relationship and celebrate their common identity as his children. Man's community with God takes shape in time: Jesus rose on the first day of the week and Christians from the beginning have gathered on that day to celebrate the fact that his resurrection changed the meaning and course of history.

The priest is present in confession as a teacher not just to inform people about the law, what the Church teaches, nor even what Jesus or Paul said. Those norms are all external, outside man. The confessor's major concern should be to make the penitent more sensitive to the guidance of the Holy Spirit who works in the depths of his heart and leads him interiorly to become a more genuine, dedicated, total Christian.

The good teacher teaches by what he says but also by the way he says it. I will never forget an incident which happened soon after my ordination. I was hearing confessions in a rural parish in a confessional on one side of the church; the pastor was on the other side. All of a sudden in the midst of a confession I heard the pastor's voice boom out, *"You what?"* I was too young and flustered to know what to do and went right on hearing confessions; but now I know that I should have asked my own penitent to excuse me, waited for the pastor's penitent to emerge, and done something on the spot to heal the pain and humiliation that person suffered. The good shepherd leaves the ninety-nine sheep and looks for the stray, and the temptation must have been very strong for that person to "get lost."

The tone of voice, the attention, the courtesy of the confessor should radiate the light and warmth of Jesus who made sinners feel at home and welcome, who ate with them and went to parties with them and did not fret that among the Pharisees he was losing his reputation.

A beginning teacher tends to teach subject matter, like English or geometry. Little by little he learns to teach people. Eventually his students teach him. Their needs and their questions force him to rethink matters he had taken for granted, and to dig more deeply into himself. Most priests in the confessional can learn quite a bit about human nature, about God and his goodness, about the deep roots and hidden power of sin—and their own need of forgiveness. After all, priests go to confession, too.

THE CONFESSOR AS FATHER

The priest in the sacrament of forgiveness should be a father, a source of life and strength, a source of correction but also support, someone who loves his child and wants to see him grow. St. Paul never hesitated to call himself a father; his celibacy set him free to beget children for Christ. The priest's title of "Father" should not be an empty phrase.

To be genuinely paternal is not to be paternalistic or patronizing. A good father does not try to keep his children dependent on him but wants them to make their own decisions, to achieve full maturity.

The model of a good confessor should be the father of the prodigal son (Lk 15:11-32). He did not just say, "I forgive you," and then go back to his business, leaving his son standing alone, isolated, without support or help. He had been watching for his son and sighted him while he was still far away. He ran out to him, embraced him, kissed him, interrupted his well-rehearsed speech, made him feel forgiven and accepted, restored his signs of rank, and threw a party to celebrate.

People used to go from all over France to confess to the Cure D'Ars. More recently pilgrims trooped down to an out-of-the-way place in the south of Italy to confess to Padre Pio who heard confessions eight hours a day. People are longing for a sign of forgiveness, a word of love. If confessions have fallen off, the remedy is to make the sacrament more what it should be: a joyous experience of God's forgiving love which calls men to change their lives and follow Christ.

SOME PRACTICAL PRINCIPLES

Perhaps the dramatic decline in confessions was needed to force a rethinking and reshaping of the way Penance is administered. If all were well, the pressure for change would be much less. Certain principles do stand out more clearly now than before.

1. Confessions should be scheduled for the convenience of the people. According to Vatican II the priest is to be there as servant. If this is not empty rhetoric, the needs and conveniences of the parishioners must come first. The Parish Council could poll the parish about the confession times they would prefer; such a question could be included in the parish census; or a survey could be taken at the liturgy on Sunday. Alternatives should be proposed, such as scheduling the Sunday Masses farther apart with time for confessions between them.

2. Frequent reminders should be given to the people about the value of confession, including confessions of devotion. A pastor of an average-sized, lower-middle-class parish regularly had the largest number of communions in his diocese. He attributed this to the 52 "spot commercials" he had prepared on communion, a different one for each week in the year. Of course quantity should not be confused with quality and frequency of confession is not an infallible gauge of spiritual progress. Nevertheless, a line or two in the parish bulletin each week, highlighting one of the special characteristics of Penance, can indicate to the people the importance of this sacrament and alert them to possibilities they may have overlooked.

If the pastor is sensitive to the problem, references to Penance will also appear often in his homilies. Scripture texts are rich in allusions to God's mercy and man's need of forgiveness, but these passages must be clarified and applied to the concrete elements of Christian life.

3. Penitents should never be rushed. Confession is a sacrament, a meeting with the God of mercy. Did Jesus limit people to 25 seconds when they came to visit him or talk to him? Yet this is the average time for confession in some parishes and even convents.

Granted that people will have to wait longer: the overwhelming majority would rather be treated personally than mechanically. This is how they discover their own dignity and God's unique concern for them. The confessional is not a vending machine.

Once the confessor begins to do this, word spreads rapidly. This frees him and the penitent from the burden of worrying what others will think when there is a very long and complicated case. Those waiting will not be tempted to leap to conclusions of any sort, for they know that they, too, will not be hurried away if they want to talk.

4. Each penitent should be taken seriously. The confessor should listen attentively and show his interest. It is unkind and counterproductive to send him off with no more than a stock phrase said to everyone. People feel hurt if someone they are talking to gives evident signs of boredom or disinterest. Each person is important to God and the priest as a man of God must manifest God's care. This may require that the confessor take a break every hour or so to get some fresh air and stay alert.

5. The confessor should feel free to ask questions: "How long has this been bothering you? What have you done to overcome it? Why do you act this way? Why is this kind of behavior wrong?"

Obviously he should not ask questions out of curiosity, nor press for details which the penitent would resent as none of his business. But sometimes the priest must uncover the inner dispositions which lie behind external actions like missing Mass, speaking unkindly of others, telling lies. He must do this not only to ease false guilt feelings caused by erroneous consciences; he must also help the sinner confront the real sinfulness of his life which often lurks beneath the surface and masks its nature with deceptive symptoms.

6. The penitent should be encouraged. Some find strength in remembering the sufferings of Christ and the saints. Others like to think of themselves as sharing Christ's ongoing campaign against evil in the world — or look ahead to their triumph with him in heaven. Still others draw hope from their own past experiences of the power of the Holy Spirit who has enabled them to win control in at least certain areas of their lives. Overcoming deeply entrenched habits can take years; the patience and confidence of an understanding confessor can enable the sinner to face this struggle day after day.

7. Absolution, the heart of the penitential rite, should be given clearly and distinctly. It is impolite for two persons to talk at the same time; if the penitent wants to say his act of contrition at the end of confession, why can't the priest wait until he finishes before beginning to absolve?

For any just cause the priest may modify and reword any of the prayers except the formula of absolution itself. For example, to emphasize or heighten the necessary dispositions, he could say, "May Almighty God (or Our Lord Jesus Christ) pardon your sins *because of your faith and your love for him.*"

The priest is now free to omit the references to canonical excommunication and interdict. Yet this is a good and logical place to remind the penitent that his sins offend not only God but the whole Church — and cut him off from the Eucharist if they are serious sins. To clarify this the confessor might say, "You have weakened the Church by your sins, but now by the authority Christ has given me I free you from whatever keeps you from full union with God's Church, and I welcome you back to the Lord's banquet of communion."

The beautiful closing prayer may also be modified by a reference to some of the situations mentioned by the penitent — indifference within the family, misunderstandings at work, sickness, loneliness: "May the passion and resurrection of Our Lord Jesus Christ, may the merits and intercession of the Blessed Virgin Mary and all the saints, may whatever good you do and whatever suffering you endure — especially your efforts at self-control and your sufferings at home— bring you the remission of your sins, an increase of grace, and the reward of everlasting life."

This prayer could be preceded by a word or two to explain that the good actions of the day are done in union with the redeeming Christ and have a value far beyond superficial appearances; the struggle against sin joins man in a special way to the suffering Savior. Such personal references are deeply appreciated by the penitent. Even a slight variation of the formula eliminates monotony, stimulates attention, and makes the sacrament a more effective sign of God's love.

8. The penance should be adapted to the individual penitent, his sins, his dispositions, his state of life. All pastoral theologians agree on this principle; but in practice the easy solution has been to assign five Hail Mary's or so many decades of the Rosary. In effect this has made the penance non-functional.

The real purpose of the penance is to reinforce the dispositions of faith, love, and sorrow and the determination to change one's life. As far as possible, the penance should begin to undo some of the damage caused by the sins confessed and to strengthen the opposite habits. An act of kindness to someone he has hurt, praise of someone he has slandered, a visit to the sick or to a neglected friend, reading a short explanation of a problem confronting him—these are practical lessons in the meaning of Christian life. If such penances are assigned with a word of explanation of why they are given, the penitent can cooperate with the grace of the sacrament with more profit.

9. Laymen and women need not wait for priests to inaugurate such changes. If they wait for the confessor to make the first move, nothing may happen. Many priests are shy and afraid of being troublesome to their penitents. Recently a priest remarked to me that he had never given absolution in English, even though it has been permitted for years, because no penitent had ever asked him to do so.

"Ask and you shall receive," Jesus said. If laymen and women want the full sign of God's forgiveness available through this sacrament, they must ask for it. They must ask for advice and encouragement. They must ask for a more meaningful penance. They must also break their own deadening routines. No longer can they be satisfied with checking sins off on a list learned long ago without any serious attempt to come to grips with themselves and the roots of their problems. They would not have spoken to Christ so carelessly, had they met him with the lepers or with Magdalen or at the healing of the paralytic or at the raising of Lazarus or the widow's son. Yet they meet the same Christ in the sacrament of Penance.

Priests and penitents, all are in the Church together. All must do what they can to make this encounter with the Lord of love a source of gratitude and joy.

To Discuss and Share with Others

1. *Have you ever felt that confession was getting to be a mechanical routine for you or your confessor? What can be done about this?*
2. *Would you prefer to have the priest talk more in confession? What would you like him to talk about?*
3. *Have you ever received helpful spiritual advice from a confessor?*
4. *Could Penance be scheduled at a better time in your parish?*
5. *Should the confessor act as a doctor? As a teacher? As a spiritual father? What would this involve?*

PART II

Formation of Conscience

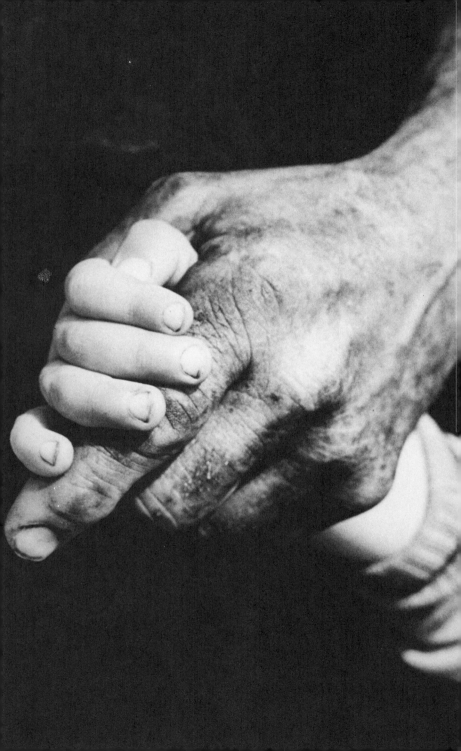

3 Affective Elements of Moral Growth

1. *Is optimism a desirable quality in a child? Why? How can it be developed?*
2. *How can parents help a child to discover God and respond to him?*
3. *What are the pros and cons of speeding up a child's religious development?*
4. *What are the signs that a child is growing in freedom?*
5. *What is the value of aggression or hostility in a child? How can it be properly channelled?*
6. *Does sex education have anything to do with religious education? Why?*
7. *How early should sex education begin? How should it be done?*

The primary school child does not suddenly develop a conscience out of the blue; this is but one stage in a whole process of moral development. To understand a child of six to nine, one must begin with infancy and briefly trace his needs and how they have been met.

Right from birth a child needs to experience constant love and affection. The very constancy and stability of love—the fact that someone is always there to hug and kiss him, to feed and change him, to wash and dry him—builds a sense of trust. The world seems orderly and reliable, and he himself must be lovable and precious since so much attention and care surrounds him.

This experience encourages the development of a positive, optimistic attitude to life, a feeling of appreciation and wonder. In an atmosphere of love the child becomes open, trustful, and ready to experiment, because he knows he will be picked up and healed should he fall and hurt himself.

Once this basic optimism is set, realism can temper it. Discipline must go hand in hand with affection, lest the child tyrannize his parents and lest his own impulses tyrannize him. The purpose of discipline is to build up in the child habits of self-control. This is an important point. The goal is not just control but self-control. Excessive control from the outside can build over-submissiveness and lay the foundations for an authoritarian personality: someone who unquestioningly obeys a command simply because it is a command. Over-control can also lead the child to doubt his own goodness—or defiantly to ignore the standards of others because they are perceived as too threatening to his self-respect. The conformist and the rebel are both products of excessive control applied by others.

More will be said about forms of discipline later. The child needs discipline to reinforce his impression that the world is orderly, and to learn that different kinds of behavior bring different results—reward or punishment.

The child should be loved unconditionally. He

should be loved for himself, not just for obeying the rules. At the same time, every genuine love is demanding. A recognizable response of love is sought, and concern for the welfare of the child includes a desire that he achieve self-mastery and freedom. In this context of love, which is both unconditional and demanding, the child can begin to discover and respond to God.

The love which parents have for their child is a share in God's creative love. God first reveals himself to the child through the tenderness and affection of his mother and the support and encouragement of his father. By around two and a half or three the child can begin to form his first vague notions of God as someone wonderful, whom even his parents respect and obey. He may have seen his parents pray, perhaps have gone to church with them, heard them speak of God's love in connection with a flower or a puppy. The child dimly perceives God's providential care and feels invited to say "yes" to him.

The child's response may be one of awe and admiration or joy and gratitude. He may be able to express it only in a smile or a widening of the eyes, in standing still or jumping in excitement. No matter. This is the awakening of his moral life under the guidance of the Holy Spirit. It is his first tentative act of love for God.

At first hesitant and unformed, this love will slowly grow in awareness and freedom until the mature person is able to commit himself without reserve to God. That point is still many years away. No one can make a gift of himself until he possesses himself, and a small child is very far from self-understanding, or self-control. But the process has started. God has begun to be recognized as good and lovable. The child has taken his first tentative steps toward God.

Wise parents will strengthen this process by calling the child's attention to God from time to time. The beauty of a clear day after a storm, the red sky at sunset, the feeling of accomplishment in speaking a new word—all of these are gifts of God, signs of his love and power.

Even more important is patience with the slow rate of development of the child. His freedom can be impaired if he is rushed beyond his own pace or if someone else's ideas or virtues are imposed on him. God does not want a child to be a carbon copy of mother or father or some mixture of both but a unique person with his own likes and dislikes.

Those values are appreciated most which are discovered by oneself, not those thrust on one by others. The child will cherish far more a weed whose beauty he has admired than some gardener's well-cultivated roses. So, too, St. Ignatius Loyola observed that there is more spiritual relish and satisfaction in mulling over a single point well understood for oneself than in looking at a whole series of beautiful ideas developed by someone else.

Few of us in fact live our lives by cultivating the hundred or so virtues described by experts on spirituality. Most Christians live on a few insights: "Love one another as I have loved you"; "What you do to others you do to me"; "To those who love God all things work together for the good." As the years go by, we find new depths in these sayings, new strength to accept setbacks and struggle forward. The same holds true for a child. The art of spiritual direction, which all good Christian parents practice, lies in discovering how God is revealing himself to this individual and what God is asking him to become.

Freedom thrives by being exercised. A child should be given many opportunities to make choices within his capacity, to experience the consequences, and to learn from his mistakes. That is how he learns to walk. It is how he makes spiritual progress, too.

Together with freedom comes responsibility—the ability to respond to the appeals of others and to do what the situation requires. Responsibility will include making up for mistakes, apologizing, asking forgiveness, repairing the damage done, and trying to do better the next time. This is all part of human life and grows easier with practice.

As the child develops more initiative, he must have adult models to imitate so as to channel his aggressive impulses into creative patterns. Boys need a clearly identifiable male as a father image; girls need a clearly identifiable female as a mother image. Women's liberation has many good points, but blurring sexual differences is not one of them. That simply confuses little children, and if parents do not serve as adult models, other adults with clear-cut work roles and identifiable uniforms will replace them—firemen, policemen, doctors, nurses, stewardesses, pilots.

It is most important that the child recognize both sexuality and aggressiveness as good, healthy, valuable elements of life so that he can develop a proper self-acceptance. Otherwise he is liable to become ashamed of what is fundamentally good and develop a false sense of guilt.

The trust and self-control learned earlier must be integrated with newly emerging powers of awareness so that he learns to cooperate and share. Proper guidance on how to express his feelings will enable him to find ways which respect the rights and feelings of others, in short, to be responsible.

A positive attitude to sexuality as a powerful force to express love and creativity will grow if the parents appreciate the goodness of the human body and freely

show their affection to each other and their entire
family.

Handling anger and frustration is in many ways
more difficult. Many people are frightened and
ashamed of their own hostility feelings and fail to
recognize their potential for good. In fact, anger is
valuable, ever necessary to human progress. Few
improvements would be made in automobiles, taxa-
tion policies, human relations, or anything else if
people did not get so frustrated that they demanded
a change.

It is normal and healthy for a child to get angry
at those who impose limits on his desires and say
"no" to him. But he can be confused at feeling hatred
for those he loves. Loving parents should remain
calm in the face of his rages and help him identify and
express his negative feelings. "You're angry, Tommy.
I understand. I know how you feel. Do you want
to pound on your drums, or would you prefer to draw
a picture about your feelings?" In this way parents
can guide the child to channel his energies into ac-
ceptable outlets like music, drawing, exercise, and
play-acting, instead of violent acts like hitting people
or throwing or tearing things. He can even put his
feelings into words, so long as they do not hurt others.
The "I hate it, but I love it" television commercial and
others of the same sort provide opportunities to discuss the matter of confusing and contradicting emotions normally felt by everyone. If the child sees that
his parents do not overreact to his expressions of hostility, that they can be sympathetic and understanding
of how he feels while they remain firm in their demands, he will be able to handle his inner turmoil
better. He can model his own self-control on what he
sees and admires in his parents.

Incidentally, it would be a mistake to introduce

Christ as a model before the child has learned to recognize, love, and admire Jesus on his own. This usually happens around age five or six. Even then Jesus should not be used as a means to manipulate the child or to get him to do what his parents want. "Eat your cereal like a good little boy. That's what Jesus would do." "Stay nice and clean like Jesus. Don't get your dress dirty." "Wash up before dinner and make Jesus happy." These are all subtle ways of associating Jesus with nagging. They earn for the Lord a low popularity rating and can poison very early any love for him.

By the time the youngster reaches school, his basic needs for security, love, and acceptance should have been met so that he is ready to develop the skills needed for success in the wider world of his peers or classmates and society in general. Now he learns the satisfaction of understanding a complex task and carrying it through to completion, the joy of using tools with ease—whether they be hammers or scissors, words or numbers. He learns to win recognition by producing things and acquiring competence.

It is crucial at this period that he experience success. He must learn that success or failure depends on the talent he has, the efforts he exerts, and the social conditions or environment where he lives. From his experience he can determine what goals are realistic for him, setting future goals a little bit ahead of past achievements so that he need never lose hope.

If a child is too often frustrated, if impossible demands are made of him, if there is no reward or recognition of his talent or effort, he can lose interest in work and take refuge in a fantasy world where success is instantaneous and utterly disproportionate to time and effort. That this predisposes him to a drug subculture hardly needs mentioning.

TO DISCUSS AND SHARE WITH OTHERS

1. *What Christian virtues do you find most attractive? Why?*
2. *What Christian virtues do you find least attractive? Why?*
3. *Do you think your attitude toward these virtues will affect your child?*
4. *Did your parents' attitudes affect you? How?*

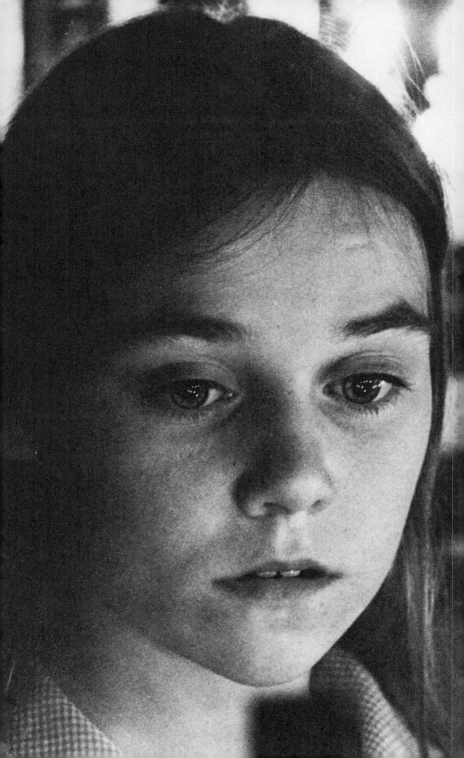

4 Cognitive Elements of Moral Growth

1. How does a child learn to distinguish between right and wrong? between sin and mistakes?

2. How early does a child begin to make moral judgments about sin?

3. How do playmates help the formation of conscience?

4. How could schools aid the development of moral judgment?

5. How should God the Father, Son, and Holy Spirit be presented to the child so as to assure a healthy development of conscience?

The emotional elements of moral development are clearly important. But even more important is growth in knowledge and judgment.

The Swiss psychologist, Jean Piaget, has charted the normal stages of moral judgment. The child first evaluates evil according to the *material damage* caused (breaking 15 cups by accident is worse than breaking one cup deliberately); then according to *punishment* or *social blame;* and finally, according to the *inner wrongness* of the act itself, taking into account subjective motives and circumstances.

When the child senses that "good" and "bad" acts

are a response to God's call to love, a "yes" or "no" to God, sin becomes possible. This usually happens somewhere around six to eight. But the child's moral judgment is still quite confused. He is capable of venial sin but not serious sin and simply cannot grasp how serious sin would be possible, since it lies entirely outside his experience.

About seven to eight the child becomes very sensitive to equality and wants everyone to be treated equally, regardless of circumstances. Motives don't count, mistakes are no excuse. As one child put it, "If a smaller child hits you, you hit him back." This fascination with rigid, mathematical equality is outgrown around 11 or 12, when justice is tempered with equity.

Around eight or nine, gangs begin to form. Children become aware of racial and religious differences, of group responsibility and loyalty. They share experiences and compare judgments. Piaget and others think that children learn the importance of motives and social consequences of behavior not through rules imposed by adults but through cooperation and conversations with their peers. Group projects in study, work, and play, therefore, have a crucial function in moral development.

Nevertheless, their moral judgment remains inadequate. For example, children before ten judge a lie which *fails* to deceive as worse than one that succeeds, because such a lie is punished. Older children reverse this judgment, for they rightly perceive the evil in lying as a violation of mutual trust.

Again, children before ten consider a lie told to an adult as worse than one told to another child; or, the bigger the exaggeration, the worse the lie, regardless of intent to deceive.

Parents and teachers can speed up the moral

progress of the child, not by skipping stages but by giving the child plenty of practice in forming judgments at each level so that he has ease and facility and feels ready to move to the next stage. After all, the young child is not judging *falsely* but *inadequately*. To break 15 dishes really is worse than breaking one—all other things being equal. But the small child simply cannot evaluate all the factors with the limited information available to him. Objective behavior is much easier for him to recognize than subjective motivation.

Furthermore, punishment or social blame can alert him to the consequences of an action. Punishment is not enough to form conscience adequately, but it can direct attention to the reasons behind the punishment.

In this connection Piaget observed that younger children simply wanted the punishment to be proportionate to the offense, though without any intrinsic connection. For instance, one should be spanked longer if more guilty. But as they grew older, they wanted the punishment to suit the crime so that they could see the reason behind the punishment. For example, a child who fails to bring back food from the market should get less food at dinner, because there is less available. He should learn from experiencing the results of his action.

Experimental evidence shows that children in Catholic schools can at an earlier age distinguish the nature and results of an action and judge independently of adults. In fact, Catholic schools are very effective in reinforcing the morality learned at home and in accelerating understanding of moral principles at an early age (eight-ten), so that the child recognizes the elements involved in making a moral decision, including elements which reduce responsibility. In other words, young children can be taught to evaluate actions according to material gravity, sufficient reflection, and full consent of the will, as we all learned when studying the catechism.

However, children below ten have great difficulty in applying those principles to themselves, that is, in making personal moral judgments about their own responsibility and guilt, in telling apart sins, mistakes, accidents, forgetfulness, and curiosity.

The stages recognized by Piaget fit readily into a more comprehensive analysis made by Lawrence Kohlberg, a psychologist at Harvard. He has detected six stages in the process of developing a mature, moral judgment. Like Piaget, he has discovered that these stages occur in a set sequence; no stage can be skipped. Some people fixate at one stage and never move beyond it. These six stages can be grouped into three general levels: pre-moral; extrinsic morality; intrinsic morality. Thus the direction of growth is to make external codes of conduct one's own by discovery of the values which lie behind the laws.

Pre-moral Level
> *Stage 1:* Fear of punishment
> *Stage 2:* Hope of reward

Extrinsic (Conventional) Morality Level
> *Stage 3:* Desire of social approval
> *Stage 4:* Respect for law and order

Intrinsic Morality Level
> *Stage 5:* Respect for the rights of others
> *Stage 6:* Appreciation of abstract principles of justice and virtue

In a crisis situation a person who ordinarily operates on a higher level of morality may regress to a lower level and find that punishment or reward are the only effective motives for avoiding sin. But to insist exclusively on fear of punishment or hope of reward as motives for behavior can stunt development at the pre-moral level.

On the level of extrinsic or conventional morality the person conforms to a set of rules, not because he knows and appreciates the reason behind the rules, but to win the praise and esteem of others (a more subtle and advanced form of reward) or out of a sense of duty. An advocate of law and order knows that laws in general are useful and valuable and obeys in a spirit of trust that the authorities responsible for the law have exercised good judgment. There is still danger, however, of a moral conformism and uncritical acceptance of authority.

On the level of intrinsic morality the person has grasped that the purpose behind the law is to protect and promote human rights. He can recognize that certain laws do not do this effectively and must be changed. When he has reached the highest stage, he has come to love and appreciate honesty, loyalty, kindness, and the other virtues for their own sake. He has practiced them and experienced their inner value. He now acts in accordance with the law, not because there is an extrinsic statute to be obeyed but because he enjoys being good. He may even have to break an unjust law out of loyalty to a higher good, as the martyrs did. Christian authors would describe this as living according to the Holy Spirit, who is an interior principle of moral behavior.

Not everyone reaches stage 5 or 6. Kohlberg thinks that fewer than 33 percent of adult Americans have attained stage 5. Nor do all reach stage 3 or 4 at the same time, though some will have arrived there by adolescence. Some people operate on stage 6 in certain areas of moral life, such as personal honesty, while remaining fixated at stage 1 or 2 in the area of sexuality or civic responsibility. Persons under stress can slip back from a higher stage to a lower, so the stages cannot be interpreted rigidly. Nevertheless, they remain very useful in charting and promoting moral growth. Experiments have shown that the best way to help a child to progress through the stages is to treat him as if he were one stage ahead of where he actually is. Children balk at operating on stages two or more degrees ahead of their present level, but respond to treatment slightly in advance of their actual development. They will try to live up to what is expected of them if it is not too far beyond their powers. Therefore, once they have reached stage 4 they should be told occasionally of the reasons behind regulations at home or school, particularly if they complain that a rule is unfair.

Unfortunately, many parents and teachers give children a distorted notion of God and of self as part of the moral development process.

God is often presented to the child as a law enforcer, to pressure the child to obey orders. God is present everywhere; he sees everything; he punishes all wrongdoing; he ceases to love disobedient sinners—so do what I tell you, or else!

Jesus Christ is presented as bringing a new law, i.e. new rules of behavior, or he seems to demand a superhuman morality. The beatitudes and other sayings from the Sermon on the Mount are considered to be a new code of precepts instead of being recognized as signs of the kingdom and a way of legitimately insisting on the need for inner morality instead of mere outward conformity.

Human nature is presented as hopelessly sinful, incorrigibly corrupt. Man's only hope would be to escape justice by an appeal to mercy—thereby eliminating any need to reform, for reform is impossible.

On the contrary, sound doctrine teaches that:

a) God never stops loving the sinner. God so loved the world that he sent his Son so that the world might be saved. God's love is stable, unshakable. In such a context, God's presence and knowledge are not threatening but a source of comfort, security, and joy.

b) Jesus Christ came to be for us a model of behavior and he gave us his Holy Spirit so that we could love one another as he loved us. St. Thomas Aquinas and moral theologians today teach that we do not get a new code of laws from Christ but an interior help to enable us to discover and fulfill our responsibilities. Jesus helps us to recognize the power of the Spirit in our lives and so have hope.

Christ as teacher is not so much a lecturer with blackboard, textbooks, and a fixed curriculum. He is more like a guru or Zen master, a man of God who reflects with us on his own life-style and helps us understand why he is the way he is and how we can be like him. He is a man of prayer in deep union with God and shows us how to deepen our own relationship with God, who sends us his Spirit as an inner principle of growth.

c) The presence of the Holy Spirit radically transforms us. Already created in God's image, we become God's adopted children, part of his family. He takes the initiative in helping us grow more and more like him, like his Son Jesus.

d) God in forgiving us does not just overlook our defects but heals us and makes us strong. We are basically good, not evil. We can trust and love ourselves; we can control our impulses and use them creatively; we need not deny their existence or fight against them, as if anger, curiosity, or sex were evil. Because each of us is good, all persons must be respected as made in God's image and called to his family. Morality should be an expression of our esteem for God and for them.

e) Good works should be prized as signs of God's kingdom, manifestations of his presence and power, not simply as giving us some claim on a reward from God or control over him. All good deeds are done with God's help and in response to his initiative. This is the meaning of that enigmatic saying of Jesus, "When you have done all you have been commanded to do, say, 'We are unprofitable servants. We have done no more than our duty' " (Lk 17:10).

Parents and teachers must accept the cognitive limitations of the child. He will misunderstand much of what they say. God may seem to him a magic wonder-worker—or at least adults may get that impression as the child tries with his limited vocabulary to explain what God means to him. Adults should not be alarmed at this; the magical stage is a normal phase of child development. Through discussion with his peers, sharing experiences and interpretations with them, he will gradually modify his ideas of God. In fact, one of the most surprising discoveries of religious child psychology is that by the age of four children have already begun to make doctrinal syntheses, which are constantly reevaluated and revised. This does not disturb the child; it should not disturb us.

Knowledge is also a very important element in self-control, especially in the ability to defer gratification, to control an immediate impulse for the sake of a future good. Such an ability is a sign that the child can make value judgments and see the relationships between present means and future goals. The sense of time needed for this develops very slowly, until by the age of ten the child has a good grasp of the near future—a few days or a week perhaps. A sense of the

distant but realistic future emerges only at adolescence.

Other skills, such as making accurate value judgments and choosing correctly can be developed earlier.
A child below ten can recognize that certain acts are
not only good for him, but good for others, too; e.g.
eating at the proper time, cooperating in games, pay-
ing attention in class. He learns that he cannot do
everything at once but must choose between eating,
sleeping, playing, working, and studying. Parents and
teachers can clarify these choices for him, remind him
of past experiences, and encourage him to learn new
values through new experiences. All this builds his
freedom.

The basic elements of Christian life—love of God
and neighbor, self-control and appreciation of values,
awareness of sin and moral responsibility—develop
very slowly. While a child may have a vague knowledge and inchoative love of the Father around age
three, he will not appreciate Christ as a model until
five or six. He becomes sensitive to the presence and
power of the Holy Spirit around seven and can recognize the help offered by the Church as his Christian
family at age eight or nine. The most important form-
ative influences throughout this process are his parents.
Their unwavering love, consistent discipline, and
readiness to forgive reveal to the child the love, justice,
and mercy of God, referred to so succinctly in the
Preface at Mass: "In love you created man; in justice
you condemned him; but in mercy you redeemed
him."

To Discuss and Share with Others

1. *Does your own experience confirm the observations of Piaget about the development of moral judgment, i.e. that there is a progress from estimating wrong according to the material damage done, then punishment and social blame, and finally interior attitudes and and motives?*

2. *Does your own experience confirm the observations of Kohlberg about the development of moral judgment, i.e. that the child moves through the stages of punishment, reward, approval, law and order, human rights, and abstract principles of justice?*

3. *Do you agree with Kohlberg that the majority of adult Americans have not reached the level of intrinsic morality? What of the public reaction to the conviction of Lieutenant Calley for the My Lai massacre? What of the glorification of the airline hijacker, D.C. Cooper? What of the conviction of Clifford Irving for writing a fraudulent biography of Howard Hughes? What of the public reaction to Supreme Court decisions? What implications does this have for American politics?*

4. *What can you do about the values of your child's playmates?*

5. *What can you do about the values taught in school?*

5 Discipline

1. Why is discipline important? What is its goal? What form of discipline is most effective?

2. What are the psychological effects of relying on physical force to control behavior?

3. How does discipline through physical force shape a child's attitude toward God and man?

4. What are the psychological effects of relying on emotional threat to control behavior?

5. How does discipline through emotional threat shape a child's attitude toward God and man?

6. What are the psychological effects of relying on reason and empathy in discipline?

7. How does discipline through reason and empathy shape attitudes toward God and man?

Discipline is one of the most powerful factors for good or ill in moral development, not only during the early years at home but also as the child moves into the wider world of school.

All forms of discipline fall roughly into three types: physical force, emotional threat, or reason and empathy.

Physical force relies on fear. It is effective for the moment, but not for long-term development, because it provokes intense hostility in the child and provides a concrete object outside himself for that hostility. It lessens his sense of being loved and his ability to sympathize with others. It focuses attention on external power rather than on internal self-control. If each fault is not punished, the child can get the impression that stealing cookies, for example, is wrong only if you are caught doing it. The greatest crime is getting caught. This is the moral code of the Mafia.

Theologically, emphasis on physical power presents God as an all-powerful lawgiver and law enforcer, the great policeman in the sky. It builds fear rather than trust, and worst of all, God's laws seem purely arbitrary: certain acts are thought to be wrong simply because God forbids them; there is no awareness that God forbids them precisely because they are wrong.

Emotional threat can take the shape of either an appeal to shame or a withdrawal of love; for example, ignoring the child, turning your back on him, refusing to speak or listen, stating dislike for him, threatening to leave him, asking why he wants to hurt you after all you have done for him.

Psychologically, this technique is very dangerous; the child perceives a loss of love as far more catastrophic than a spanking. A small child with little sense of time may think the withdrawal of love will last forever. Like physical punishment emotional threat can be effective for the moment, but not for long-term moral development. It produces anxiety and disproportionate guilt feelings, attacks the child's sense of self-respect and self-worth, distorts his ability to sympathize with the one injured, and fails to highlight the real reasons for good behavior.

Theologically, emotional threat reduces love to power and to a bargaining relationship: "I will love you if you wipe your feet, keep quiet, eat your spinach, do what I say." On the contrary, God never stops loving even though the covenant has been broken by sin. God does not trade his love, he gives it freely.

The third type of discipline relies on *reason and empathy*. One explains the physical and emotional reality of a situation, the harmful effects to self and others. One appeals to the child's sense of self-respect and self-mastery, his desire to be grown-up, his concern for others, their needs and desires. The hostile behavior of others is explained.

All this builds on the child's limited but growing ability to understand the situation, to control his own impulses, and to appreciate the feelings and rights of others. It integrates his emotional empathy with knowledge of the consequences of his behavior. This heightens his sensitivity to the reasonable elements in the situation and enables him to generalize from his experience so that in the future he can foresee the consequences of his acts and develop a healthy and appropriate sense of guilt if he does wrong. Empathy, building on the emotional basis of love, intensifies the motivation to control impulses.

Theologically, this correlates with the redemptive incarnation of Jesus Christ. Jesus knowingly and willingly identified himself with mankind and healed our wounds by his self-sacrifice. He overcame our refusal to love by loving without restraint, giving us an example of service to others at the cost of pain to himself.

Research shows that a combination of reason and empathy is the most effective form of discipline. Still, one should not expect even the most effective training to influence behavior mechanically, for the human person remains free. But proper discipline does consistently influence attitudes; i.e. awareness of responsibility and a sense of guilt for doing wrong.

Of course, evaluation of any discipline techniques must take into account the total emotional relationship between the child, his parents, siblings, teachers, and peers; past practices and self-esteem of family members; the social and economic status of the family; the influence of TV and neighborhood as well as school. Nevertheless, of all these elements the parents are the most important. They influence the moral development of the child by meeting his needs for security and affection, by providing a context of consistent discipline, by encouraging the development of skills through experience of success, and also by acting as models to admire and imitate. If they themselves have experienced the satisfaction and rewards of success, if they consistently control immediate impulses to achieve future goals, if they retain their hope and create an atmosphere of love, if they express easily their confidence in God and their gratitude for his presence and providential care, the child will have what he needs for proper growth.

TO DISCUSS AND SHARE WITH OTHERS

1. *What advantages and disadvantages of physical punishment have you experienced yourself?*

2. *What advantages and disadvantages of emotional punishment have you experienced yourself?*

3. *What advantages and disadvantages of reason and empathy as a form of discipline have you experienced yourself?*

PART III

Children And Confession

6 The First Confession

1. *When do you think a child should be taught about sin? How should this be done?*
2. *How can children learn to examine their consciences?*
3. *How can parents best introduce a child to prayer?*
4. *How can television, Mass, and the bible be used to help in developing an awareness of sin and God's readiness to forgive?*
5. *How can parents find the right kind of priest for first confession?*
6. *What qualities should he have?*

Within the broader background of the religious and moral development of the child a more specific preparation for the sacrament of Penance should be made.

SETTING THE SCENE

The growing child should learn that God not only loves him and gives gifts to him, but that God wants a response of love. He wants the child to think of him, talk to him, and give signs of love, like being kind, sharing clothes and toys, and obeying parents and teachers.

Parents can help by creating an atmosphere of prayer from time to time in which the child can be especially sensitive to God's presence and love. Some parents like to pray with their children before bedtime, reading a bit of scripture perhaps, thanking God for the specific joys of that day, telling him of their worries and plans, expressing their reliance on him, asking pardon for faults. Others may prefer to do this at mealtime, or occasionally throughout the day. The important thing is that it be regular and frequent, so that the children accept this as part of life.

If prayer attunes the family to God's presence and love, each one can share God's attitude to oneself and to the others. In such a context of prayer it is easier to accept oneself with all one's weaknesses and faults and to become aware of the never-ending struggle to be better, a struggle in which one can count on others to help.

If the family recites prayers together, it is essential that the meaning of these prayers be explained. A child whose mentality is magical in its early stages of growth can all too easily get the impression that prayers are magic formulas, that one must know the right words in the right sequence to get results. This can be avoided if father or mother paraphrase difficult prayers in words the child can grasp. When prayers like the Our Father or the Act of Contrition are paraphrased or explained, there is a perfect opportunity to draw attention to God's will that we grow and overcome our human shortcomings.

Children like to learn fixed formulas. They use them in their clubs and at play. They want their parents to use them at home. Such formulas give them a sense of security and familiarity. Prayer formulas can be useful, then, as long as they are short, simple, and in a language with which the child feels comfortable. At the same time, there should be enough depth to the prayer so that it will not be set aside later as "childish." Adults should be able to use it, too. Here is an example of such an act of contrition:

O my God, I have sinned.
I am sorry. Please forgive me.
I disobeyed you and hurt others.
I deserve to be punished.
But I know you love me,
and I want to love you more.
With Jesus' help
I will try to make up for my sins
and stay away from all that leads me to sin. Amen.

The first two lines suffice for very young children. When they are ready for their first confession, they can learn the rest.

The references to sin and forgiveness at Mass may be called to the child's attention, particularly if he has begun to attend regularly and is already familiar with some of the parts. Mass begins with an admission of guilt and an assurance of God's pardon. The readings from the bible or the homily may refer to sin and God's mercy. And just before Communion at every Mass mention is made of the need for forgiveness; the Our Father, kiss of peace, and Lamb of God all bring out the fact that the Eucharist is a meal in which we are reconciled with one another as well as with God. Jesus draws all his brothers and sisters closer together as they move closer to him.

The child should be reminded that the right attitude and dispositions are needed before approaching our Lord in Holy Communion. He must be sorry for his own sins and ready to forgive others. Then he, too, will be forgiven when Jesus comes to him.

Children best learn of the existence and importance of the sacrament of Penance from going along when their parents confess and seeing its importance and effects in the lives of adults. Some parents have found it worthwhile to mention the penance assigned by the priest, to explain its purpose, and to invite their children to help them fulfill it. Children like to feel responsible for their parents and the mutual support knits the family together.

Periodically parents might read to their children New Testament stories of sin and pardon to see how they react. Luke's gospel is full of such incidents: the Good Shepherd (15:4-7), the Prodigal Son and forgiving father (15:11-32), the ten lepers (17:11-19), Zacchaeus (19:1-10), the sinful woman (7:36-50), the son of the widow of Naim (7:11-17), the paralytic (5:17-26), eating with sinners (5:29-32). John's gospel is particularly vivid on the forgiveness offered to Peter by the risen Christ (John 18:15-27; 21:15-17). Such stories can form deep impressions about God's mercy and readiness to forgive, about the power of Christ and the role of priests in the sacrament of Penance.

It may help to analyze a television show with the children now and then. What makes the villain a villain? How does he reveal his attitudes in his gestures, tone of voice, facial expression, words? Why are his actions bad? Why is he punished? Is this punishment fair? How does the hero show that he is good or at least trying to improve?

Westerns are particularly useful for this kind of discussion. They are our morality plays. Some situation comedies like *All in the Family* also convey a strong moral message, but they are usually too sophisticated for a small child to follow.

Analyses of Westerns and crime programs can readily lead into a discussion of the need to apologize and how this is done: tears, downcast eyes, bowed head, shaking hands, giving gifts. Forgiveness does not do away with the need to make up the damage done, to return what was taken, and to try to do better.

It is useful to point out that being sorry, admitting guilt, asking pardon, and being forgiven can actually bind a group more firmly together, whether it be a family or team, a group of playmates or schoolmates. They accept one another more realistically, despite their faults, and the free quality of their love stands out more evidently.

A meeting between parents and religion teachers will give them a chance to compare notes on whether the child is ready to confess. The could talk over sections of the religion text which are directed to sin and penance. They might also discuss how the parents could best prepare their children for the sacrament, and how to reinforce what they have learned in class.

Introducing Children to the Sacrament

One of the most important contributions a parent or teacher can make is to find a good confessor for the children. He need not be from their parish; one is free to confess to any priest. Whatever time and trouble are spent in locating him and arranging for first confessions is a very sound investment. First impressions are lasting, and children need someone who establishes rapport with them easily, is not bored by their faults, but patient, interested, and understanding, and knows how to give suitable advice. Such confessors are rare.

If the children do not already know the priest, arrange a preliminary meeting where they can get to know and like one another. Anonymity is usually not so precious to children as familiarity. That someone cares enough to recognize them can be a sign of God's personal concern for them.

The first confession need not take place in a confessional. For a reasonable cause, another suitable place may be used, and some children might feel the strangeness of the confessional quite distracting and even fearful. Many priests prefer to start children off in the sacristy with both a kneeler and a chair for the child, while the priest sits with his back to the sacristy door. The child then can choose to kneel behind the priest and remain unseen or sit in the chair facing him.

In any case, well before his first confession the child should be given an opportunity to explore the confessional: to see where the priest sits; to work the slide; to find the location of the kneeler, ledge, screen, and doorknob; to get used to the darkness. This is a good time to explain the secrecy of confession, and that the priest will never reveal his sins to anyone. The darkness is an apt symbol of this. Some children find the darkness and anonymity attractive. It may help them overcome their initial shyness. They may want to confess "just the way" adults do. Their wishes should be respected, the choice is theirs.

The child should not be overwhelmed with intricate details and ceremonies for his first confession. They can easily distract his attention from the central points—awareness of sin, sorrow, telling his sins to the priest, and following the priest's advice.

Examination of conscience is best done at first by thinking of different familiar places—home, school, playground, street, church—and trying to remember whether they were good or bad there, whether they loved others and helped as they should. Lists of sins can be harmful for young children. For some children such lists suggest new sins or lead to scruples. For others they foster a habit of conformism and passivity, leaving moral decisions to others instead of developing sensitivity to God's call to love. Few lists are suited to the ever-shifting mentality of the child; as a result they can encourage a merely superficial self-understanding.

The child need not worry about getting the correct words to describe his sins. He can just explain things in his own way. He should be encouraged, though, to tell *why* he sinned and *how* he plans to improve in the future.

A party after first confession intensifies the joy which should surround forgiveness. It shows that others, too, are happy at the sinner's reconciliation with God. The whole Christian community, but especially his family and friends, are glad that he has taken a step forward toward maturity. All those who had a share in the preparation process and the ceremony itself should be invited: parents, teacher, children, and priest.

The Role of the Confessor in First Confession

As was mentioned above, the child should be given a choice whether to confess in a confessional or elsewhere, anonymously or openly. Canon law simply says that the confessional is the *proper* place, not the only place. The excitement connected to first confession certainly constitutes an excusing cause. But the decision should be left to the child. Of all the sacraments Penance is the least structured, and right from the beginning the child should be given a chance to experience his Christian freedom in moral matters.

The confessor should be sensitive to the feelings of children and aware of how important their first confession is to them. A great deal of tact is needed to ask enough questions to show personal interest without asking so many that the child becomes upset or anxious.

A very young child cannot profit from much advice. He will forget it anyway. But he can benefit from a reassurance that he is good and that God loves him. Encouragement to be kind, to pray, and to try to control himself in order to please God will usually meet a ready response.

Because a young child cannot commit serious sin, there is no need to insist on the exact species and number of his sins. In fact, a general confession has many advantages. It lessens the tensions of examining a conscience whose attention span and memory are so short. It makes an informal conversation much easier. It shifts the focus from the external action to the motive and the general attitude of loving obedience.

Insistence on completeness and exactitude would make the child worry and prepare the way for scruples. After all, these are confessions of devotion. Great freedom should be encouraged so that the child can experience God's forgiveness as a source of peace and joy.

On the other hand, if a child wants to give unnecessary details, the confessor should accept the fact that they are important to the child. Often no one listens to the child at home. How marvelous that he has become someone important in this sacrament! Full attention is given to him here. Besides, a child's thought processes are concrete. It is far more natural for him to say, "I didn't set the table" or "I didn't watch my baby sister" than "I was disobedient."

Such details often help the confessor find an imaginative penance. To recite the "Our Father" or "Hail Mary" can be counterproductive. Such a penance often is performed either thoughtlessly or scrupulously and may well reinforce a magical attitude toward the sacrament. Far better to pray in his own words for someone he hurt. Better still, an act of kindness that the offended one would appreciate—to dramatize the genuine sorrow and desire to improve.

In the early Church one of the signs of forgiveness was the laying of hands on the head of the penitent. This gesture could still be very meaningful and impressive to children. After hearing the confessions of the children privately, the confessor could come out, sit on a suitable chair, and give absolution to each child while laying on or at least stretching out his hand over each child's head in turn.

Confessions for children should not be a deadly routine but a joyous experience that God loves them, forgives them, and sends them off to do better. Forgiven sinners left Jesus full of joy; so will the children leave the confessional if they have met there the God of love.

To Discuss and Share with Others

1. *Can you remember your own first confession? What stands out in your mind? Why?*
2. *When do you think you first committed a sin? What did you do about it?*
3. *What kind of an attitude do you have toward Penance now? How does this affect your child's attitude toward the sacrament?*
4. *Should children make their first confession the same way as adults confess?*

7 When Should Confession Begin?

1. *At what age should a child begin to confess? Why?*
2. *How can penitential celebrations prepare children for confession?*
3. *Do you think the average good Christian commits mortal sin often?*
4. *At what age would you explain mortal sin to a child? Why?*
5. *How can religion class help the formation of conscience after first confession?*
6. *How can the confessor help the formation of conscience during childhood and adolescence?*

Confession should begin when the child is aware of God's call to love, of his own sinful refusal to respond, and of his need of pardon. He should also appreciate the special qualities of the sacramental sign of forgiveness, be able to profit spiritually from confession and freely desire it for himself. Finally, the benefits should outweigh any potential harm.

FREEDOM OR FORCE?

Many religious educators feel that very early confession should not be positively encouraged. Nor should it be discouraged. Children should be left free to decide for themselves when they want to confess. There should be no pressure either way.

Vatican Council II in its *Declaration on Religious Education* (No. 1) insisted that children should be helped to acquire a more mature sense of responsibility toward pursuing authentic freedom, embracing moral values by personal choice. The same idea was repeated and expanded in the Council's *Declaration on Religious Freedom* (No. 8). This principle of freedom must be applied to all the sacraments, for in them man lovingly, and therefore freely, encounters God. This is particularly true of Penance which is nothing else than man's exercise of freedom.

But more than freedom is involved. The *Constitution on the Sacred Liturgy* (Nos. 11, 14) states that "the faithful should take part fully aware of what they are doing, actively engaged in the rite." The Council also directed that both religious education and the liturgy be adapted to the psychology of children and others.

How can these principles be put into practice? How can confession be made as fruitful as possible? How can Penance be made attractive without forcing children to confess?

We must stop herding children to confession before Communion. This puts undue psychological pressure on them. No one is obliged to confess unless he has committed a serious sin, and moral theologians generally agree that children below ten are incapable of mortal sin; they do not have enough understanding of the consequences of sin or enough self-possession and self-control to make the kind of decisions which would forever destroy all their love for God.

On the other hand, no one may forbid a child to confess or refuse to absolve him. By six or seven a child is capable of committing venial sins. If he wants to confess them, he has a right to the sacrament. Church authorities have properly insisted that his right be respected.

THE ROLE OF SCHOOL

In the first grade the primary focus of religion classes should be on God's personal and reliable love. Prayer and kindness to others are positive responses to God. Sin is saying "no" to God, refusing to respond as he wants. Jesus reveals God's love and shows us how to respond to the Father.

Punishment should be mentioned only as a sign of God's love and a call to be sorry. Otherwise there is great danger that a child may mistakenly think that God ceases to love him when he sins. Examples can show that punishment at home is a sign, not of rejection, but of love. And God is even more ready to forgive than most loving parents.

In second and third grades the children are still in a dawning awareness of their own personal moral life. A few are moving beyond what Kohlberg termed the pre-moral life of reward and punishment to a morality of conformity to laws and rules. They can grasp something of the drama of sin as invitation and refusal and of the drama of redemption as repentance, pardon, and grateful joy. They can reenact parables and incidents from the bible which illustrate this and can make up similar stories and plays of their own.

But children of seven to nine are not yet capable of mortal sin and cannot really understand terms like mortal sin, venial sin, original sin, actual sin. They memorize the words, but their significance lies outside their experience and they seriously misinterpret them. Hell as eternal damnation can have no meaning except terror until children are old enough to understand mortal sin personally, since mortal sin is the tentative beginning of hell on earth. A God who would send anyone to hell appears merciless and cruel to young children. What is important is not so much what is taught, but what the child *thinks* is being taught. For a child with an immature conscience, unending punishment will present a distorted image of God which may remain with him throughout life.

By seven or eight most children are capable of venial sin and repentance. They should be taught that forgiveness comes through asking God's pardon, showing love to others, and receiving Jesus in Holy Communion.

They should also learn that Jesus comes to them in a special way in the sacrament of Penance to assure them that God forgives them and wants them to grow. They should be taught how to confess and given opportunities to receive absolution if they wish.

PENITENTIAL CELEBRATIONS

Religion class affords an excellent opportunity to teach the social and ecclesial aspects of sin and forgiveness by communal celebrations of various sorts.

The purpose of these celebrations is to awaken an awareness of sin and a spirit of penance. Different ceremonies can highlight different aspects of God's love, man's selfishness, the effect of sin, God's readiness to forgive, the rich symbolism of the sacrament, the demands of true repentance, and the joy that follows forgiveness. Through these the child can learn better how to examine his conscience and plan for the future. Their aim is not primarily to instruct, however, but to provide a religious experience in which the children can discover themselves and Christ on a whole new level.

Classroom, schoolyard, and church can serve as appropriate settings and tie in these places with a sense of God's presence and the children's responsibility to him. Occasionally such celebrations could be held in homes in the neighborhood for small groups of families and friends.

Appropriate times would be the liturgical seasons of Advent and Lent as well as the beginning and end of the school year. These form part of the rhythm of life and afford natural opportunities to look back over the past and plan for the future.

The basic structure of a penitential celebration is quite simple: an examination of conscience preceded or followed by some readings from the Word of God about love and sin; an expression of sorrow and amendment; confession and absolution (if the sacrament is to be received); an expression of mutual joy.

Communal celebrations should at first be non-sacramental, until the children get used to the format. They will be more impressive if carried out leisurely and with a certain degree of solemnity. The readers should speak slowly, clearly, and with feeling so as to heighten the religious atmosphere. All of this demands enough advance preparation and rehearsal so that the songs and readings and responses do not distract the children but enhance the effect. As far as possible, music and light, procession and gesture should be integrated into the ceremony.

For example, the celebration could begin with an entrance song and a procession to the vestibule of the church or baptismal font. This movement can subtly call attention to man's movement away from God by sin and his need to return to God and to the community. If the number present is too large for this, they could at least leave the pews and stand in the aisles—

an uncomfortable position, calling for change.

After a word of welcome, the priest can invite the people to be seated and listen to the Word of God. The scripture passages and responses from the Lenten Masses offer an abundance of material on love, sin, sorrow, and mercy. Other readings from the new breviary, *Prayer of Christians,* or other sources could be added.

A brief homily emphasizes one of the elements of the sacrament of Penance and situates it within the life of the Church. The social dimension of sin, the concern of the whole Church for sinners, the relationship of Penance to some other sacrament particularly relevant to this group could be indicated.

The homily is followed by a brief period of silent reflection. If the penitents are old enough to profit, they could split into groups to discuss the meaning of God's Word for their life together and perhaps reach some decisions on what they could do jointly to improve their situation.

The resolutions emerging from discussions could be read aloud or some other form of examination of conscience, confession of fault, resolution to amend, and petitions of God's mercy could be used. A series of prayers in the form of a litany is often effective.

Along with the Act of Contrition there should be some sign of mutual forgiveness to dramatize reconciliation with the Church as well as with God. The penitents could shake hands during the Act of Contrition. If the group is small enough, they could gather around the altar and place their hands on it as a gesture of covenant renewal. Or the lights in church could be put out while they carry lighted candles to the altar; in the combined light of many candles they can see one another and the altar clearly. Children also enjoy being sprinkled with holy water as a reminder of the cleansing effects of baptism and penance.

Individual confession and absolution should be introduced into the celebration at this point when the children are old enough to profit from the sacrament— usually around third grade. In some places a general absolution is given after individual confession to bring out more clearly the communal aspects of God's forgiveness. If this is done, care should be taken that children old enough to sin seriously know of the obligation to confess mortal sin. Otherwise they might get the impression that no more is required than the general accusation of faults in the common ceremony. It is true that one is excused from detailed confession of mortal sins if time or circumstances make it impossible, but such sins should be confessed later at a convenient time.

After absolution the group may perform a common penance, like reciting a prayer or singing a hymn. Some priests simply accept the sign of mutual forgiveness which preceded confession as the penance, as was the custom in the early Church. Others consider as penance the carrying out of the resolutions for group action to remedy abuses. This has the advantage of extending the sacramental penance over a longer period, reminding the group of the need for mutual support.

The celebration should end on a note of joy, often expressed in song. A party or the Eucharist could follow.

CONTINUING FORMATION OF CONSCIENCE

Whether Penance is begun in the setting of a communal celebration or in the confessional, formation of conscience must go on, for children of eight or nine are still very far from a mature sense of responsibility and sin. Young children tend to project into the past their growing awareness of sin, with the result that actions done in innocence may lead to deep feelings of guilt later on.

Teachers and parents should be careful not to interpret the actions of children in the light of their own mature consciences. They must demand no more of them than they are capable of at the moment.

As soon as the children can grasp the difference, clear distinctions should be made between temptations, accidents, normal behavior, and sin. God wants the children to see and accept themselves as he sees them—a mixture of good and bad, but still lovable. He wants them to appreciate and improve their good points as well as to struggle against evil.

Parents and teachers should never use God as a law enforcer for them, to avoid discipline problems: "God will punish you if you don't stop hitting your sister." "It's a sin to watch television after your bedtime." "Sit down and keep quiet or God will not love you." Not only are such statements bad theology and untrue, they can permanently distort the children's attitude to God.

How often should a third grader confess? As often as he wishes. Certainly he should have the opportunity to receive the sacrament in connection with a penitential celebration three or four times a year. His parents should also invite him to accompany them as often as they go to confession privately. However, he should never be forced to confess. It is probably best if he does not confess every week at this stage, for there is danger of forming a habit of routine, superficial examination of conscience.

By fourth grade children have a natural concern for law and order. They play games with complicated rules rigidly enforced. They are creatures of habit and easily adopt set patterns of behavior. This provides an opportunity to develop Christian virtues. But the dangers of moral conformism must be met by emphasizing the importance of motive and attitude. God wants not just outwardly correct behavior, but love.

Fortunately, children now become more interested in the reasons behind a law. No longer do they accept rules or standards of behavior on parental authority. They are beginning to feel a conflict between codes of behavior learned at home and those of their classmates. This makes it possible for them to have lively discussions of laws and rules. They can discover and appreciate values by reflecting on their own experiences and on the programs they watch on television.

Unless they begin the habit of confession now, it may become very difficult in the next few years to overcome their sense of shyness and shame, especially if they think they are committing sexual sins.

At this age, too, attention span increases and children can profit more fully from personal advice and encouragement from the confessor. The habit of frequent confession can be explained and safely encouraged. Now most children begin to enjoy confession. Some of them want to identify themselves or even confess outside the confessional. They should know they are free to choose whatever confessor they wish.

A wise and patient confessor can get the nine-to-ten year old to look beyond the external act to the interior sinful attitude. He can ask why he got into fights or disobeyed, and how he will try to do better. There is really no effective substitute for this personal guidance in the formation of conscience.

A confessor can clarify the dynamics of temptations, the difference between temptation and sin, and techniques for overcoming temptation. Children frequently feel ashamed when they are tempted. They may feel guilty because they had strong feelings of hatred or jealousy. It is good to remind them that temptation is part of human life, that Jesus Christ was tempted. Actually, temptation offers an opportunity to renew and intensify loyalty to God. It is never a sin unless we freely consent to do what we know is wrong. Discussion of these points in religion class will enable the teacher to encourage the children to discover for themselves the advantages of frequent confession as a help against temptation.

Many moral theologians think that children become capable of serious sin around this age. At least they can understand what mortal sin involves and often overestimate the gravity of their offenses. Therefore they should be carefully instructed in the three elements of serious sin: grave matter, sufficient reflection, and full consent of the will. As they learn through confession to apply these criteria to their own behavior, this will free them from false guilt feelings.

Fifth grade is the time to present Penance as the sacrament of freedom and hope. Children of ten or 11 can appreciate that the priest in confession is like a father who wants to understand or like a doctor who wants to heal them. It is not enough to tell the doctor, "I'm sick. Something's wrong." They must describe their symptoms as fully as they can and take the medicine he prescribes.

They can also begin to analyze sample confessions of adults and learn how to improve their own:

"Forgive me, Father. I'm a married man. It's been a month since my last confession. I got angry and lost my temper at the children. This happens often now when I get home from work. I'm tired and

I don't want to be bothered.

"I know this is selfish. My anger just makes things worse. I'll try to spend more time with the kids and listen to them instead of yell. Where should I start? Have you any advice?"

Children can learn much from such a confession. The man described not just his sins, but the pattern: when and where they happened, and how often. He looked for reasons why he acted that way. He planned how to change. He asked for advice.

Once they have the feel of it, children can role-play confessions of their own, one taking the part of the priest, another that of the penitent. Practice confessions like this can lead into very fruitful discussions about spiritual progress.

Around this age children like penances specially designed for them. If the priest can't think of an imaginative penance, he can always ask the child. One time I asked a little girl what she would like to do to make up with her mother. "I'd like to bake a cake," she said.

"Can you really bake a cake?"

"Yes, Father."

"Would your mother like it?"

"Oh, yes."

"All right, for your penance bake a cake for your mother."

When I think of the mess in the kitchen, that might have been more penitential for the mother! But it was a chance to let the child express repentance in her own way. And she certainly remembered it a lot longer than she would have remembered a "Hail Mary"! Cleaning up the mess together probably brought her and her mother much closer and taught far more effectively than any words that the little girl's moral growth was the responsibility of them both.

Fifth and sixth graders will not participate so readily in penitential celebrations. But the confessor can alert them to the social and ecclesial dimensions of sin and penance, reminding them of the damage to the Church done by sins, of the prayers offered for them by others, and of their own responsibility to live as good Christians to bear witness to Christ.

Around sixth grade, children become more sensitive to the influence of good or bad example. This provides a starting point to discuss original sin and the cumulative impact of sin in the world. They can appreciate the Old Testament on a much deeper level than was possible previously.

Preadolescence is a period of idealism, when the children often daydream and identify with heroic models like Christ and the saints, especially the martyrs. They can begin to appreciate the suffering and misunderstanding inseparable from trying to live a good life in a sinful world. They can recognize the crucifixion and death of Christ as a sign of love but also as a revelation of the inner dynamics of sin. Now is the time to mention the need to confess every serious sin, and to confess later any serious sins which were forgotten.

With the onset of adolescence there is a return from the objectivity characteristic of the nine-to-twelve year old to interiority and introspection. Factual information is less interesting to the adolescent than self-understanding. Formation of conscience about love, human relations, work and leisure, justice and peace takes precedence over doctrinal clarity.

The adolescent in modern society is exposed to a welter of conflicting values. He needs wise and sympathetic guidance as he tests these values and makes them his own. He will be very critical of those who do not live up to the values they profess. So his spiritual life will often fluctuate between bursts of enthusiasm and periods of deep dejection and self-doubt as he becomes more aware of the extent of his own sinfulness.

Confession becomes very important to provide spiritual direction during these crises and to do away with false fear and shame. Scruples, too, can plague the adolescent and drive him from God. He must be reminded again and again of God's love, of the strength God offers, of his own basic goodness. Passions are powerful drives to good, once they can be controlled. While the struggle for control goes on, the important thing is to keep trying and never lose hope.

Action becomes a prominent part of adolescent formation of conscience. Values will be more appreciated and retained if discovered in action and expressed in action. Group cooperation to shape society according to the values they share can be very effective.

Adolescents will get more out of communal penitential celebrations if they are the climax of a prolonged experience; e.g., something could be planned for a football team at the end of a season, or for a class at the end of a semester. If a group of teenagers gather for a weekend retreat, communal penance will be more effective on the second day, after a psychological buildup. Some groups have a community meal after the penance service; during the meal no one is to serve himself but must look after the needs of others. Such experiences bind the group more closely together.

WHAT ABOUT CONFESSION BEFORE COMMUNION?

Certain parishes and dioceses still encourage first confession before first Communion. A brief discussion of the pros and cons in dialogue form may clarify matters.

"Without confession the child might receive the Eucharist unworthily." This fear is not well-founded, because there is general agreement among moral theologians and pastoral psychologists that a child below ten usually does not have enough maturity of conscience to sin mortally, certainly not at six or seven.

"Yet a young child can commit at least subjective venial sins. Why should he be deprived of the sacramental sign of forgiveness?" Indeed he should not be refused absolution if he wants to confess; but he should not be forced or pressured into it. He should also be made aware of the many other ways venial sins are forgiven. Too early confession can obscure the value of these normal elements of Christian life: prayer, acts of charity, self-denial, Holy Communion.

"Little children speak about their sins and faults willingly and openly. Is this not then the best time to train them to be honest and frank in confession?" This is a shrewd observation. But there is plenty of time to begin confession after first Communion and still take advantage of this openness, which lasts until nine or ten.

"Around six or seven the child is very sensitive to the symbolism of the liturgy. By nine or ten he is less interested in spiritual meanings than in the effects produced. A spirit of objectivity and legalism can replace his desire to be good out of love for God." This is true, and it is why the child should be introduced to the rich symbolism of penitential celebrations in

second or third grade. These prepare him to appreciate the sacramental signs of private confession in
third and fourth grade.

"Why not begin confession before Communion to
help form a sensitive conscience?" Sensitivity of conscience can be developed in many ways better adapted
to the limited understanding of the child.

"Yet children begin at an early age many practices
they don't understand; why not Penance?" Vatican
II in the *Constitution on the Sacred Liturgy* states,
"Pastors of souls must realize that, when the liturgy is
celebrated, more is required than the mere observance
of laws governing valid and licit celebration. It is
their duty also to ensure that the faithful take part
knowingly, actively, and fruitfully" (No. 11). Besides, going through a ceremony he does not understand can give a child the impression that religion is
a matter of external words and actions, the very thing
that Jesus and the prophets complained about.

"Doesn't early confession lay the foundations of
regular confession later on? Without it, won't the
children neglect the sacrament of Penance?" Quite
the contrary. It builds subconscious resentment of a
habit imposed from outside, before the child is psychologically ready for it. When pressure to confess is
removed, as for example during the summer or when
the child leaves Catholic school, the habit is not con-
tinued; confessions cease. But even when they con-
tinue, the habit is often a bad habit: They have developed scruples and false consciences, accusing themselves of mortal sin when no sin at all exists "just to
be safe." This makes it much more difficult to have
genuine sorrow over real sins.

"But surely we should not deprive children of the
grace of the sacrament?" Granted, but grace is received according to the disposition of the penitent. A

young child does not have the psychological substructure to be so disposed for the sacrament that he can profit from its frequent use for the remission of venial sins. He lacks the maturity of conscience needed before the unique value of *confession* as a means of forgiveness can be appreciated.

Experience in the confessional has convinced many pastoral theologians that early confession—before first Communion—is harmful for many if not most children. Their moral development becomes stunted, fixated at what Kohlberg terms the pre-moral or conventional morality levels. Adults go on confessing that they missed Mass even though they were sick because it makes them "feel better," this is a sign that they are using the sacrament to relieve guilt feelings rather than confront real guilt.

Because their understanding of the sacrament and their ability to profit from it is so limited, young children easily fall into a habit of superficiality and careless routine—a perfunctory examination of conscience, a few words in the confessional, a hastily murmured prayer, but no serious efforts at reform.

Even worse is the development of a magical attitude to confession. The mentality of little children is magical rather than causal. In their world of make-believe certain words or actions produce magical effects. Applied to Penance such an attitude means that the exact recitation of a formula frees the child from the need to have genuine sorrow, to struggle against sin, or to repair the damage he has caused. It also produces disillusionment and despair when no real change occurs despite repeated confessions.

WHY NOT BEGIN CONFESSION AT ADOLESCENCE?

To avoid the dangers of premature confession,

some have suggested postponing Penance until around
13. They feel that below that age a child can't really
love, can't sin at all, can't profit from the sacrament,
and would be positively harmed by it.

According to them, only fully mature love is
worthy of the name of love, a love of others for their
own sake; such a love is possible only at adolescence.
This view does justice neither to the findings of psychology nor to moral theology. Kohlberg estimates
that only about 13 percent of the boys at age 13 have
moved beyond conventional morality; few adults
would consider teenage love "fully mature." In fact
love, like life, develops gradually and moves through
stages. It is mere playing with words to say that a six-
year-old child does not love his parents—or God.

But can a child really sin before adolescence? A
handful of authors say "no" on the theory that venial
sin is not possible before mortal sin and that mortal
sin is impossible before adolescence. They would forbid confession to a preadolescent on the grounds that
absolution would be invalid. But the overwhelming
majority of moral theologians agree that venial sin is
possible before serious sin, and indeed psychologically
predisposes man toward it. Relying on experience,
they insist that children below puberty do sin. Their
sense of sin is still incomplete, as is their sorrow for
sin. But it is present and can be intensified by the
sacrament when the child is able to engage in a meaningful and fruitful dialogue with the priest.

The strongest argument of those who favor post-
ponement is that a child who learns about Christian
penance in the "pre-moral" context of rewards and
punishments or the "conventional" context of precepts
and prohibitions has learned about it inadequately
and therefore incorrectly; and that such misconceptions are very hard to dislodge. It is true that some

misconceptions about penance resist reeducation. But there is little if any evidence that these are due to beginning confession at ten instead of seven. Just because understanding is inadequate, it is not necessarily incorrect or erroneous; it is correct as far as it goes. It will be corrected as more is learned. And proper reception of Penance can advance the learning process.

If confession is not begun before puberty, the natural teenage embarrassment and antipathy toward authority will make reception of the sacrament rare. Even adult converts find confession difficult, no matter how much they appreciate the value of the sacrament in theory. The solution to misconceptions about Penance is not to postpone the sacrament but to remedy abuses in the way it is received and to reveal the values of confession as soon as they can be experienced and appreciated.

Confessions should be neither forced nor forbidden but freely chosen. At all times formation of conscience must stress freedom and autonomy. The children gradually become aware of themselves as free. The more that parents, teachers, and confessors respect and promote that freedom, the better. Christianity is a religion of love, and all true love is freely given.

TO DISCUSS AND SHARE WITH OTHERS

1. *There are many people with scruples. Do you think that improper preparation for Penance can lead to scruples? Why?*
2. *How often should a child confess? Why?*
3. *How often should an adolescent confess? Why?*
4. *What are the reasons for and against beginning confession before first Communion?*

Bibliography

De la Cruz Aymes, Maria, F. J. Buckley, and Cyr Miller, *New Life,* Vols. I-IV, Sadlier, N.Y. 1971-1972. An illustration of how a religious education program can form consciences gradually.

——————, *On Our Way,* Vols. I-VI, Sadlier, N.Y. 1966-1970. De la Cruz Aymes, Maria, F. J. Buckley, and Vin Fallon, *In The Spirit,* Sadlier, N.Y. 1969. A booklet to help parents form the consciences of children.

Buckley, F. J., *Children and God:* Communion, Confession, Confirmation, Corpus, N.Y. 1970. Provides the scholarly references to much of what is contained in this book.

Corrigan, John E., *Growing Up Christian,* Pflaum, Dayton, 1969. Practical guide to the moral development of children.

Ginott, Haim, *Between Parent and Child,* Macmillan, N.Y. 1965. Excellent practical suggestions to improve parent-child relations.

Flavell, J. H., *Developmental Psychology of Jean Piaget,* Van Nostrand, Princeton, 1963. A good introduction to Piaget.

Lee, R. S., *Your Growing Child and Religion,* Macmillan, N.Y. 1966. Psychological approach to maturity.

Lehmeier, Ludwig, *The Ecclesial Dimensions of the Sacrament of Penance from a Catechetical Point of View,* Cebu City, Philippines, University of San Carlos, 1967. Particularly valuable for sample Penitential celebrations.

Sloyan, Gerard S., *How Do I Know I'm Doing Right?* Pflaum, Dayton, 1966. A simple introduction to modern developments in moral theology.

Strommen, Merton, editor, *Research on Religious Development,* Hawthorn, N.Y. 1971. A collection of articles summarizing recent research, some of which deals with moral development.

Freburger, William, *Repent and Believe,* Ave Maria Press, Notre Dame, Ind., 1972. A good collection of examinations of conscience and communal Penance services.